LITT

PASTA

THE LITTLE BOOK OF PASTA

Text by Stephanie Buick

An Hachette UK Company
www.hachette.co.uk

Summersdale Publishers Ltd
Part of Octopus Publishing Group Limited
Carmelite House
50 Victoria Embankment
LONDON
EC4Y 0DZ
UK

www.summersdale.com

Printed and bound in the UK

ISBN: 978-1-80007-841-3

The LITTLE BOOK OF PASTA

Rufus Cavendish

Contents

LIFE IS A COMBINATION OF MAGIC AND PASTA.

Federico Fellini

Introduction

Pasta is one of the world's most versatile and most universally loved foods. Perhaps you've always got a pasta stash in your kitchen cupboard and you are already adept at putting together a sumptuously layered lasagne to share with family and friends. Maybe you have fond holiday memories of sitting outside a bustling trattoria in Rome, forking up twirls of tomato-smothered spaghetti sprinkled with black pepper and tangy fronds of parmesan cheese. Or maybe you've been lucky enough to taste the divine delights of sweet, pumpkin-filled ravioli and you're keen to make them yourself.

In this little book of pasta we will take a brief look at the history of this simple flour-and-wheat staple. We'll explore the stories behind some of those intriguing pasta shapes and the classic pasta sauces. Finally, we'll round off with a selection of truly mouth-watering recipes, ranging from the very simple to the more elaborate. So, if curling up with a steaming bowl of your favourite pasta transports you to your happy place, read on.

A BRIEF HISTORY OF PASTA

For thousands of years people have cultivated wheat, ground it into flour and combined it with water to form dough. This dough has been pulled, twisted, rolled, stuffed, boiled, baked and fried to make a huge variety of foods. So we find, for example, noodles in China, udon in Japan, pierogi dumplings in Eastern Europe and, of course, pasta, which the Italians, in particular, took to their hearts and made their own.

Many of the myriad pasta shapes and accompanying sauces were created in Italy and it would be unthinkable for pasta to be absent from any Italian restaurant menu.

But pasta has an ancient history, not all of it straightforward. Some of it is surprising and much of it is open to speculation.

Where did pasta originate?

It's a commonly held belief that the famous Venetian explorer and merchant, Marco Polo, brought noodles back along the Silk Road from China to Europe and that the noodles evolved from there into the pasta we know today. It is certainly true that in his book, *The Travels of Marco Polo*, he referred to a tree, most likely the sago palm, that produced a starch which the Chinese processed into noodles. It's also probable that he did bring some of these noodles back with him. It is thought, however, that the story of him introducing pasta to Europe was part of an advertising campaign for a Canadian spaghetti company during the 1920s and 1930s, and that this story is easily debunked by earlier references to pasta-like foods. Food historians, for example, have mentioned a Genoese soldier who listed "a basket of macaronis" among his possessions. This was in 1279, nearly twenty years before Marco Polo returned from China.

Ancient Greek and Roman texts refer to *lagana*, a flour-and-water dough rolled into thin sheets then dried out on a hot stone. Sometimes these were pepped up with spices and the juice of crushed lettuce then deep-fried to produce a crispy pancake. Not everybody could afford spices though, so the sheets would often be sliced into thin strips and boiled or added to vegetable and legume stews to bulk them out.

Lagane were such standard fare for poor people they even get a mention from the Roman poet, Horace, who wrote a satirical piece about his pauper's life, including his eagerness to get home to a humble bowl of leek and chickpea broth with lagane. Today, the simple but wholesome dish of lagane and chickpeas is still popular in southern Italy.

The earliest visual reference to pasta was unearthed by archaeologists in an Etruscan tomb near Cerveteri, north-west of Rome. This bas-relief of a pastry board, rolling pin and cutter is thought to date back to the fourth century BCE.

The development of pasta in Italy

In 827 CE, Arabs from North Africa landed on the sun-baked Mediterranean island of Sicily, at the crossroads of North Africa and Europe. It's thought that they were the first people to dehydrate wheat products for preservation on long sea voyages.

During their two hundred years of occupation, they had a major influence on the cuisine, introducing citrus fruits, artichokes, sugar cane, spinach and aubergines. Sweet flavours such as citrus fruits, raisins and fennel still appear in Sicilian pasta recipes.

The Arabs also introduced durum wheat to Sicily and southern Italy. It grew well there and, in the Naples area, the sea breezes and hot winds generated by Mt Vesuvius were perfect for the freshly made pasta hanging outside to dry.

Severe famines had afflicted the country through the ages, but now dried wheat staples such as pasta and couscous could be produced in greater quantity and then stored and transported. By the fourteenth century, Genoese sailors were taking dried pasta from southern Italy to the north.

When extrusion machines that pushed the dough through dies to produce different shapes were invented in Naples during the seventeenth century, large-scale production of dried pasta really took off. Pasta became the street food of the people, so much so that Neapolitans were known as *mangia-maccheroni* (macaroni eaters). *Maccaronaros* (macaroni street vendors) cooked it over a charcoal fire and it was eaten by hand with grated sheep's or goat's cheese.

Meanwhile, the wealthier parts of northern Italy had been experiencing the Renaissance, a period characterized by a resurgence of interest in classical antiquity, in particular with regard to philosophy, music, art and architecture. This drive for artistic perfection included a surge of interest in sophisticated foods and elaborate presentation, and pasta, the humble street food, reached lofty new heights when it found its way into the sumptuous banquets of the prosperous.

Pasta, in all its forms, became an everyday food for everyone from the very rich to the very poor, and when Italians later began to migrate in large numbers to other countries, they took this simple yet versatile staple with them.

DID YOU KNOW?

The tomato is central to southern Italian cuisine but it was only introduced to Italy during the mid-sixteenth century, perhaps when Cosimo I, a leading member of the Medici family, married the Spanish princess Elena di Toledo.

This elite union probably resulted in the introduction of other tasty culinary imports such as chocolate, coffee and chillies, which had been taken back to Spain from the New World.

But the tomato, a member of the deadly nightshade family, was regarded with great suspicion by the Italians. Nicknamed "the devil's fruit", it didn't become an everyday staple until the nineteenth century.

I AM NOT ONE
TO TURN DOWN
MACARONI AND CHEESE,
EVEN LATE AT NIGHT.
I LOVE ITALIAN FOOD.
I LOVE PASTA.

Queen Latifah

How did pasta become a global dish?

Pasta has travelled far and wide and much of this is due to waves of Italians seeking opportunities abroad. During the nineteenth century, poverty, malnutrition, disease and poor farming forced many southern Italian families to emigrate. Between the mid-nineteenth century and the 1920s, more than four million Italians left for the Americas, followed by another wave of people fleeing post-war poverty after the Mussolini dictatorship.

Many Italian immigrants chose to start their new lives in New York. Dried pasta was easy to import and Italian-run eateries sprang up all over the place, enabling Italian communities to socialize and eat food that reminded them of home.

From these eateries new dishes emerged, such as the creamy alfredo, which was quite unlike any pasta dish eaten in Italy. Similarly, spaghetti and meatballs, which were never eaten together in Italy, became popular among Italian immigrants in the US where meat was more affordable and more readily available.

During this time, successive waves of Italians also emigrated to the United Kingdom. The first pasta factory in Britain opened in 1936 but it wasn't until the late 1950s that pasta restaurants began to open, mostly in London.

In most UK households, however, pasta was still seen as an exotic food until air travel became popular during the 1960s and 1970s. The popularity of foreign holidays among the sun-starved British grew and as more people travelled to Italy and enjoyed the cuisine, they brought those tastes back home. The demand for pasta increased, and canned versions, such as spaghetti hoops, tinned ravioli, spaghetti bolognese and Alphabetti spaghetti, started to appear on supermarket shelves. More Italian restaurants opened their doors and, with time, pasta dishes gradually became commonplace in the UK. As with the US, some of the classic recipes evolved into dishes that would be unrecognizable in Italy. The cream-smothered carbonara, for example, and the mince-laden "spag bol" are now everyday favourites in the UK.

THOMAS JEFFERSON

The third president and principal author of the Declaration of Independence did much to increase the popularity of pasta in the United States. In 1784, Jefferson, a great food lover, had been dispatched to France as a diplomatic agent, and after travelling around France and northern Italy, he developed a taste for fine dining. During a trip to Naples he fell in love with pasta and, on returning to the US, he prepared a large shipment of culinary goodies that included almonds, raisins, parmesan cheese, anchovies, tarragon vinegar, many crates of pasta and a pasta-making machine. He made copious notes on the workings of the machine, on how to make pasta and the best kind of flour to use, then went on to serve macaroni and cheese to dinner guests. Pasta was already available in a few places in the US, but by the end of the eighteenth century it was being imported from Sicily. Following the opening of pasta factories in the US from the mid-nineteenth century, it became much more widely available.

A brief history of pasta shapes

Ridged, ruffled, tubed, long, short, plump or skinny. There are over six hundred different pasta shapes of varying lengths, diameters and contours. These range from the simple to the complex to the truly flamboyant, such as the ruffle-edged campanelle, and the unashamedly playful, such as racchette (tennis racquets), orecchiette (little ears), radiatori (radiators), alphabet letters and dinosaurs.

While some pasta shapes have cute or funny stories behind them, the pairing of specific shapes with particular sauces is considered by pasta lovers to be a very serious business. The convolutions and hollows of the more complex shapes provide spaces for the sauce to pool, and the larger surface area enables each piece to grip more sauce. As the great Italian cookery writer Marcella Hazan said, the importance of pairing pasta and sauce "cannot be ignored by anyone who wants to achieve the full and harmonious expression of flavour of which Italian cooking is capable".

Strozzapreti

Strozzapreti, "priest stranglers" or "priest chokers", is the name for a type of pasta from the Emilia-Romagna region in the north of Italy. From 756 to 1870, the Church controlled this area as one of the papal states. The Pope, who was feared by all, introduced heavy taxes, and forced people to hand over additional money that, he assured them, would redeem their sins and buy them "a place in heaven". Not only did the Church take ownership of land, rivers and roads, but also the clergymen, notorious for their gluttonous ways, would regularly help themselves to farm produce such as milk, cheese, meat and eggs. To add insult to injury, they would then invite themselves into people's homes expecting to be fed. Housewives would have to prepare food with the few ingredients they had left so the obvious choice was pasta, made only from flour and water as the eggs had been confiscated. From this situation, strozzapreti was born: lengths of egg-free pasta, around 6 cm long, twisted like a rope and thickened in the middle.

There are a few stories behind the name, all based on the overwhelming resentment towards the Church. The pasta shape was thought to resemble a clerical collar, or "priest choker". It's also possible that people talked with glee about the priests shovelling the pasta down so fast they would choke. It's easy to picture the housewives bristling with resentment, uttering curses under their breath as they twisted the pasta, imagining – or hoping – it would get stuck in the throats of the greedy clergymen.

Nowadays, free of Church tyranny, the popularity of strozzapreti persists, and as well as the classic strozzapreti there is a gnocchi version: strangolapreti. A hearty strangolapreti, made with stale bread, parmesan and spinach, is found in the Alpine region of Trentino-Alto Adige, and the Umbrian version is made with spinach and ricotta cheese.

All of these types are substantial and the twisted shape creates extra space for sauces to cling to. They work well with thick sauces like ragù or those containing chunks of meat or vegetables.

Common pasta shapes

PENNE

ORECCHIETTE

CONCHIGLIE

BUCATINI

RUOTE

CAVATAPPI

FUSILLI

FARFALLE

SPAGHETTI

PIPE RIGATE

MACARONI

RIGATONI

LASAGNE

AVEMARIE

PIPETTE RIGATE

CANNELLONI

PAPPARDELLE

RAVIOLI

GNOCCHI

CRESTE DI GALLO

STELLE

FIOCCHI RIGATI

RICCIOLI

TORTIGLIONI

GEMELLI

PIPPE DOPPIA

GARGANELLI

TAGLIATELLE CORTE

IF I START FEELING DOWN I'LL GORGE MYSELF ON PASTA. THAT USUALLY DOES THE TRICK. IT'S THE ITALIAN BLOOD IN ME.

Natalie Imbruglia

Pasta ripiena – filled pasta

The northern regions of Tuscany, Emilia-Romagna and Lombardy are home to the very versatile pasta *ripieni*. They come in a wide range of shapes and sizes from the dainty little tortellini twists, to the larger and more functional ravioli and may be served with a sauce or simply heaped in a bowl and smothered with melted herb butter.

These stuffed pasta shapes became popular during the fifteenth century at the start of the Renaissance when they were presented by *Bartolomeo Scappi*, a celebrity chef of his time. He created flamboyant banquets for the elite – the aristocracy and top members of the clergy – who were keen to show off their wealth.

It was around this time that pumpkins were introduced to Italy, prompting Scappi and other top chefs to experiment with complementary sweet ingredients such as rosewater, cinnamon, ginger and nutmeg. Some of these even found their way into savoury pasta fillings.

Eventually, as with so many foods considered to be the domain of the elite, these appealing pasta shapes, so time-consuming to make yet so pretty and so satisfying to eat, filtered down to the general population, who would often cook them in broth and usually reserve them for special occasions such as saints' days and Christmas.

They are still widely eaten today, and the fertile northern region of Italy produces such an abundance of fresh ingredients that ripieni can be stuffed with just about anything: tender ham, minced beef, soft cheese or fresh herbs.

Sweet ingredients, such as pumpkin, fruit or honey, are also popular, and the sweet-savoury combinations that emerged during the Renaissance are still enjoyed today, over five hundred years later. In particular, the tangy *mostarda di frutta* – fruits preserved in the seemingly unlikely combination of sugar and mustard oil – are used in ripieni. This filling is particularly popular at Christmas and is a speciality of these regions, with each town producing its own variety.

TORTELLONI – LITTLE PIES

Tortelloni are formed by placing a filling, traditionally ricotta cheese and spinach or basil, on circular, rolled-out pieces of dough that are then folded in half. The ends of each piece are brought together, rather like circular croissants. Tortellini, the smaller version, usually contain meat.

Tortelloni are sometimes called *ombelico di Venere* (navel of Venus). According to legend, the goddess Venus stayed at an inn halfway between Bologna and Modena. The landlord, after catching a glimpse of her navel, was overcome by her beauty and was inspired to create a pasta in that shape.

CAPPELLETTI – LITTLE HATS

These small ripieni from Emilia-Romagna, similar in shape to tortelloni, are eaten in broth on Christmas Day. For many families, getting together to knead the dough, cut it, fill it and twist it into shape is a special tradition. The cappelletti can be filled with a variety of ingredients, depending on family preference.

RAVIOLI

"Ravioli" derives from the old Italian word *riavvolgere*, meaning "to wrap", lending weight to the theory that it originates from Genoese sailors who wrapped their food up inside squares of pasta.

Just to complicate matters, however, a medieval Italian cookery book refers to an Arab recipe from 1100 for *sambusak*, a meat-filled pasta triangle similar to the samosas we have today. This has led to speculation that filled pastas may have been introduced to Italy by the Arabs. It is not clear, therefore, whether the recipe was brought into Italy via the trade routes or whether it was introduced during the Arab occupation of Sicily.

Today's square-shaped ravioli bears little or no resemblance to these early recipes for stuffed pasta. Traditionally it was filled with cheese, herbs and egg, and then served in a broth. Today it is often stuffed with meat, although seafood ravioli dishes have also become popular.

Gnocchi

Gnoccho means lump. Technically, gnocchi are dumplings, but as they regularly appear on the menus of Italian restaurants and in pasta cookery books, this much-loved comfort food deserves a mention here. These flour and potato dumplings hail from northern Italy, and while they are substantial and filling there is nothing lump-like about their texture, which is light and fluffy.

The Spanish brought potatoes from Peru to Europe during the sixteenth century, but this new crop was treated with mistrust by Italian farmers for some time, so it wasn't for another hundred years or so that potatoes were used to make gnocchi. Instead, flour or breadcrumbs were combined with cheese, and sometimes eggs. Chestnuts, rice, barley and stale bread have also been used.

An indulgently rich variation is *gnocchi alla romana*, made with a dough of semolina, hot milk, parmesan cheese, egg yolks and butter. It is cut into discs and baked in the oven until soft and cheesy on the inside and crispy on the outside.

Fazzoletti di seta – silk handkerchiefs

These delicate sheets of pasta fall into silken folds when dropped onto the plate. They are made in the same way as lasagne but the sheets are rolled out much more thinly and many modern chefs cut them into free-form shapes. Fazzoletti originate from the Liguria region, where they are often made with white wine and flour. They are thought to have emerged as a result of the bustling trade routes between ancient Europe and China when silk was one of the most commonly traded goods. The Romans loved silk so much that they would drape it decoratively in their windows, and over their balconies, their furniture and their bodies. It is easy to see how this love of silky textures extended to this culinary creation. This ultra-thin tissue version of lasagne would have been served with equally delicate accompaniments such as ricotta with cinnamon or *prescinsêua*, a sour Ligurian cheese that is a cross between ricotta and yogurt. Much later, in the mid-nineteenth century, it was paired with pesto.

Tubular pastas

Tubular pastas allow the sauce to coat the inside of the tube as well as the outside.

MACCHERONI (MACARONI)

All pasta used to be referred to as maccheroni. This might be because the Latin *maccare* means to knead. Also, the ancient Greeks used the word *makaria* for any food made of barley. Later, barley was substituted for durum wheat and makaria became maccheroni.

A childhood favourite for many of us, often associated with cheese sauce, this dish has endless variations that can be created by adding ingredients such as mushrooms or truffle oil. Hunks of ham or smoky Spanish chorizo sausage, beer or chillies give the dish an exciting kick.

BUCATINI

A thick, hollow spaghetti, often paired with one of the classic Roman quartet of sauces (page 40). This pasta might need some taming if you want to wrap it round your fork without splattering yourself with sauce.

FUSILLI CON BUCO

Originally made by Neapolitan women who'd wrap a bucatino around a knitting needle. The extra spirals result in sauce-hugging nooks and are great for thinner, oily sauces, such as tomato.

ZITONI

These fat, rough-textured tubes are traditionally eaten at celebrations. The whole family could join in snapping the pasta lengths. Zitoni are eaten with *ragù alla napoletana*, which is similar to the ragù from Bologna but uses tomatoes and whole pieces of meat instead of minced.

PENNE/RIGATONI

These shortish, chunky tubes are popular in Roman restaurants. Rigatoni are straight-cut, ridged and wider than penne, which are cut diagonally and may be smooth or ridged. Perfect for strongly flavoured sauces such as tomato, and robust enough to support any creamy or meat sauce.

Orecchiette

In the heel of Italy lies the region of Puglia, where ancient, crumbling towns meet the turquoise sea and where holidaymakers flock to see the fairy-tale-like *trulli*: white conical buildings with domed roofs. It is here that the small pasta pieces known as *orecchiette* (or "little ears") originate, although they are enjoyed all over Italy. It is believed by some food historians that they were taken to Puglia from Provence in France during the thirteenth century by the Angevin dynasty.

The concave shape of orecchiette is formed by a firm roll of the thumb, resulting in an inner thumb print and rough outer surface that enables the pasta to hold a lot of sauce. Small orecchiette are served with a ragù or small meatballs in a tomato sauce and a sprinkling of ricotta. Larger orecchiette are served with vegetables, in particular cime di rapa (turnip tops), broccoli or cauliflower, which have been sautéed in the olive oil for which the region is famous.

DID YOU KNOW?

During the eighteenth century, young, aristocratic English men, known as "dandies" because of their fashionable appearance, would commonly undertake a grand cultural tour of Europe. They would return laden with flamboyant clothes and exotic foods, including macaroni, which they adored so much that they would describe anything fashionable, such as their fine clothes or ultra-high, bouffant hairstyles, as "macaroni".

The American War of Independence was taking place during the same period, and the English liked to poke fun at the Americans, hence the line from the song, "Yankee Doodle Dandy": "stuck a feather in his cap and called it macaroni".

DID YOU KNOW?

In the South American countries of Argentina, Paraguay and Uruguay, it is considered good luck to eat gnocchi on the twenty-ninth of every month. Some eateries will even feature a "gnocchi special". When families and friends come together for this tradition, the host will leave a coin or bank note under their guests' dinner plates.

PASTA IS THE ONE FOOD I CAN'T LIVE WITHOUT.

Joe Bastianich

Key pasta dishes

RAGÙ ALLA BOLOGNESE

A city with endless medieval colonnades and two leaning towers, Bologna is often called, *La Dotta, La Grassa, La Rossa*, meaning "The Learned, The Fat, The Red" after its ancient university, love of food and red rooftops.

It is from this bustling student city, that *ragù alla bolognese* originates. Chopped or minced beef and pork are browned in the same pan and gently simmered in wine, tomato purée and *soffritto*: finely chopped onions, carrots, celery and pancetta that have been gently cooked in butter or oil.

Traditionally, garlic is not used and, apart from the occasional bay leaf or sprig of rosemary, herbs are not usually included either. Instead, these basic ingredients are allowed to speak for themselves by the slow-cooking process that creates a rich meaty sauce, usually served with tagliatelle or used as a base for lasagne.

PIZZOCCHERI

This short, chunky tagliatelle-like pasta is believed to come from Valtellina, in the mountainous area close to the Swiss border in the northern region of Lombardy. Here, it's too cold for wheat to grow so other carbohydrates such as rice and potatoes are eaten instead. For pasta, buckwheat is used, although sometimes wheat flour is added for flexibility and strength. Pizzoccheri are used as the main ingredient in thick stews, which also tend to be referred to as pizzoccheri.

These stews typically consist of potatoes, garlic and a mix of green leafy vegetables such as Swiss chard, cavolo nero or Savoy cabbage.

Generous dollops of butter and chunks of hard cheese also find their way into the cooking pot and the whole lot is baked in the oven to create a delicious, stick-to-your-ribs dish, hearty enough to warm the heart (and stomach) of any mountain dweller.

PESTO

On the northern Mediterranean coast of Italy, in an area known as the Italian Riviera, sits Genoa, an ancient and busy trading port with magnificent squares and a warren of alleyways. It is said that the most delicious basil in Italy, with its small, tender leaves and sharp taste, grows in the hills west of the port. In the past, basil leaves were harvested during the summer and preserved in oil for the winter months, enabling the people of that area to make use of this distinctive flavour all year round.

This probably explains why Genoa is the birthplace of pesto sauce. "Pesto" comes from *pestare*, from the Genoese dialect, meaning to pound or beat, and is related to the word pestle, harking back to Roman times when pounding ingredients together using a wooden pestle and marble bowl was a very simple and common way of combining food ingredients.

Pesto is still made in this way today. Pine nuts and garlic are pounded together, followed by fresh basil leaves and generous quantities of olive oil. Finally, a strong cheese such as parmesan or pecorino is added to create an oily, dark green sauce with an interesting, nutty texture and a hit of salt that is tempered by the creaminess of the cheese.

The combination of flavour profiles created by ingredients of this kind is nothing new: the Romans prepared a paste called *moretum* that consisted of garlic, salt, cheese, herbs, olive oil and vinegar. During the Middle Ages, crushed walnuts and garlic was a standard dish in this area. Later, pine nuts from the forests along the coast of the Tyrrhenian Sea were introduced, as was basil, when spice traders brought it back from India and South East Asia. Pesto was eaten with large, very thin squares of pasta, but today it is usually served with a chunky pasta that will hold the sauce, such as penne.

The classic Roman quartet: cacio e pepe, gricia, amatriciana and carbonara

The inhabitants of Rome, the Eternal City, who adore pasta, pride themselves on simplicity and authenticity in their cuisine. From glossy restaurants to bustling back-street trattorias, chefs prepare these four unshakeable favourites with speedy efficiency, energetically tossing the ingredients together in small frying pans.

This culinary equality wasn't always the case. Throughout history, a huge gulf in wealth meant that the peasant classes were forced to cook meals from a very few, simple ingredients. Curing meat and coating it in herbs preserved it during the colder months but also enhanced the taste.

Centuries later, this region of culinary traditionalists still holds simple but tasty cooking close to its heart, in particular, cheese, cured pork and pasta.

There are over a hundred different cheeses in the

Lazio area and cured meats are still immensely popular. But it is guanciale and the sheep's cheese, pecorino, that are the key ingredients of Roman pasta dishes. Spaghetti, bucatini or rigatoni are the pastas of choice because their bulk allows them to stand up to these robust sauces.

CACIO E PEPE

This is the simplest of the Roman dishes and contains just three ingredients: cheese, black pepper and pasta. Some recipes call for the sharpness of pecorino cheese, while others combine it with parmesan for an extra salty kick.

GRICIA

This is the most ancient of the Roman quartet and is thought to have originated around 400 CE in the mountainous region inland from Lazio where shepherds would eat fried guanciale (cured pork jowls or cheeks) with pecorino cheese. These dry foods, rich in protein and fats, would have been perfect for the shepherds who needed to spend days at a time in the mountains. This food combination later becomes known as gricia.

AMATRICIANA

Like gricia, this features the combination of guanciale and pecorino cheese, but in the town of Amatrice in northern Lazio, in the late eighteenth century, tomatoes and chillies were added, bringing acidity and heat to the dish, and from this amatriciana emerged.

CARBONARA

This contains the same ingredients as gricia but with egg yolks stirred in to give it extra richness. While the history of carbonara is unclear, it has been suggested that the name comes from *carbone* (charcoal), which was used for cooking by woodcutters in mountain areas, and that the specks of black pepper represent the charcoal.

What is certain, however, is that those who could afford it at some point incorporated eggs into the gricia recipe, enriching the flavour, adding substance and volume and enhancing its nutritional value.

In some countries, in particular the UK, copious quantities of cream have found their way into carbonara, resulting in a richer, much sloppier dish, an adaptation that strikes horror into the hearts of Italians.

Which pasta shapes go with which sauces?

With an array of sauces to choose from, and an abundance of pasta shapes, there are seemingly unlimited possibilities for pairing the two.

These recipes include specific suggestions for pairing pasta shapes and sauces and while there are no set rules, it's worth thinking about the combination you use.

- **Long thin pasta shapes** work well with oily sauces or those containing fat-based ingredients such as pancetta.

- **Delicate shapes** such as fettucine go with lighter sauces, for example a white wine-based sauce.

- **Chunky pastas** like bucatini or penne go with chunky meat sauces or those with lots of cheese.

- **For thin sauces** such as a light tomato and basil, choose shapes with nooks and crannies that will trap the sauce, such as farfalle.

Sugo alla puttanesca

The name of the dish from Naples known as *puttanesca*, "in the style of the whore", originates from the word *puttana*, or "whore". There are a number of explanations for this rather surprising appellation, for some of which we can look to the word itself.

Compared with other pasta dishes, puttanesca is relatively modern, having emerged from Naples during the Second World War when food was scarce, poverty was rife and women sometimes resorted to prostitution simply to feed their families.

Puttanesca contains tomatoes, oregano and black olives, together with a tangy trio of chillies, capers and garlic. It has been suggested that the strong smell of this dish would have enticed men in from the street, although the fundamental flaw with this idea is that they would have been looking for food rather than an encounter with a prostitute.

An alternative theory is that the women needed something that they could prepare and eat quickly between customers; or perhaps they even made this dish for the men to eat.

Another explanation comes from the way in which Italians use the word as a general catch-all to mean "stuff" or "bits and pieces". This certainly sums up the recipe, with its throw-anything-in set of ingredients. Lending weight to this theory is the story of a restaurant on the island of Ischia in the Gulf of Naples. Late one night, a group of hungry customers asked the owner to rustle up a meal. The harried owner complained that the kitchen was bare, so the customers asked him to sling together whatever he had to make *puttanata qualsiasi* (literally, "whore whatever"). And so tomatoes, capers, anchovies and olives formed the basis of the sauce that night.

Sauces containing some or all of these ingredients are popular in the Naples area, in particular *aulive e chiappariell*, i.e. olives and capers. As is typical with sauces in this part of Italy, puttanesca is most commonly served with spaghetti.

DID YOU KNOW?

Tunisia comes second to Italy in terms of their annual pasta consumption.

Spaghetti and smaller shapes such as macaroni are the most popular, with the name *makarona* being a catch-all for any pasta shape.

Makarona is usually cooked in the same pot as the sauce. Tunisian pasta sauces are usually tomato-based and, in keeping with Tunisian cuisine, are seasoned with spices and cayenne pepper to create a one-pot dish that is rich, tasty and blow-your-socks-off hot.

The versatile and much-loved makarona works equally well with chicken or with red meat such as beef or goat, and with legumes such as lentils or chickpeas.

THE STRANDS OF SPAGHETTI
WERE VITAL, ALMOST ALIVE
IN MY MOUTH. IT'S HARD TO
BELIEVE OLIVE OIL, PASTA,
GARLIC AND CHEESE COULD
MARRY SO PERFECTLY.

Ruth Reichl

MAKING THE MOST OF YOUR PASTA:
Cooking Tips and Tricks

The idea of pasta-making may conjure up images of white-hatted, floury-armed restaurant chefs bristling with enthusiastic efficiency. In your own kitchen, however, kneading together the simple ingredients of flour and water can be a calming experience that ramps up to creative fun when you start rolling, cutting, crimping and twisting that unassuming ball of dough into shapes.

A food processor and pasta machine will speed up the process but they're not essential. The beauty of home-made pasta is that it requires just a clean work surface, a rolling pin and a knife. This simplicity leaves you free to experiment with different shapes, fillings and ingredients.

In this chapter we'll feature some basic methods for making your own pasta and we'll also explore the key ingredients used to create those delectable sauces.

Tips for cooking pasta

Al dente, meaning "to the tooth", means firm to the bite without being crunchy. This traditional way to cook pasta takes longer to digest than soft-cooked so you stay full longer. But there are no rigid rules and you may prefer yours softer.

The following steps will help you to serve up beautiful pasta to your own taste.

- **Get everything else prepared first:** Set your table and have side dishes ready. Don't be tempted to cook your pasta first: it could soften and clump together while it's sitting around waiting for the sauce.

- **You probably need more water than you think:** The pasta pieces need space to move around and expand while they cook. Six litres per 500 g of pasta is a good guideline.

- **Never add oil to the water:** Oil clings to the pasta and stops the sauce adhering to the surface. A good stir when you drop the pasta in the pan and a few more during cooking will be enough to stop it sticking.

- **Your cooking water should contain enough salt to make it "taste like the sea":** This old quote is sometimes disputed but salt enhances the taste of pasta: 1 tbsp of salt for every 3 litres of water is the recommended amount. This may seem a lot but your pasta only needs a maximum of 10–12 minutes (fresh pasta even less) so it doesn't have time to absorb much salt. Apart from bringing out the flavour of the pasta, salt toughens the surface slightly, preventing it from becoming slimy.

- **Add a splash of pasta water to your sauce:** The starches in the water will help the sauce cling to the pasta.

- **Ensure the water is boiling properly before you add the pasta:** When you add the uncooked pasta, the water temperature drops so a larger quantity of boiling water will allow it to retain its heat and quickly come back to the boil. For delicate shapes such as ravioli, reduce the temperature a little while you add the pasta.

- **Make sure you know the recommended cooking time for your pasta:** Dried pasta takes longer to cook than fresh, and thin shapes like tagliatelle cook more quickly than chunky ones such as penne. Cooking times also vary from one brand to the next so always look at the instructions on the packet. Check the pasta 2 or 3 minutes before the recommended cooking time is up; this will allow you to cook it to your own taste.

- **Shake it well when you drain it:** Pasta can retain pockets of water, especially shapes that are dimpled or folded. Delicate shapes only need a gentle shake.

- **Do not rinse:** The starches in the cooking water stay on the surface of the pasta and help the sauce cling to it.

- **Serve immediately after draining:** Do not leave it to dry as this can result in the pieces sticking together.

FRESH OR DRIED PASTA?

And so this long-standing debate continues.

The most commonly held opinion is that fresh pasta is somehow superior to dried. Fresh pasta has a softer texture and, some might argue, a more satisfying flavour.

But dried pasta has its advantages too: a much longer shelf life, making it convenient to transport and store, and a sturdier dough, enabling it to be formed into complex shapes. A sign of a good-quality dried pasta brand is the marking, *pura semola di grano duro*, meaning, "pure durum wheat semolina". *Trafilata al bronzo* on the label indicates it has been extruded through a machine with a bronze die. Bronze-die extruded pasta has a rougher surface texture, enabling it to grip the sauce better.

If you're buying ready-made pasta, it's worth bearing in mind that neither type is superior to the other; they are just different. So weigh up the characteristics of each and buy the one that best suits your needs.

DID YOU KNOW?

World Pasta Day is on 25 October. The first World Pasta Congress was held in 1995 when 40 pasta producers came from all over the world to gather in Rome. Luigi Cristiano Laurenza, head of the International Pasta Organisation, said, "The central goal of World Pasta Day is to call attention not just to the product of pasta, but to new, healthy and creative ways to enjoy a pasta meal."

IT ACTUALLY TAKES
QUITE AN EFFORT
TO MAKE POOR
LINGUINE POMODORO.

Anthony Bourdain

Types of flour for making pasta

Because flour is the main ingredient in pasta, the type you select will greatly affect the flavour, strength and texture. This is where gluten comes in. Gluten is a protein that gives pasta its elasticity and firmness so flour with a high gluten content will produce pasta dough that is easier to knead, roll out and form into shapes.

The mixing and kneading process makes the dough firm and elastic. Leaving the dough to rest after kneading improves elasticity because it allows the gluten bonds to strengthen. Using eggs or egg yolks in your pasta will weaken the gluten and make the pasta more likely to break so it will need careful handling, especially if you're making filled pasta shapes such as tortellini.

To help get you started, here is a quick guide to the different types of available flour, including gluten-free options.

- **Semolina/durum wheat flour:** This is one of the most commonly used flours for making pasta, and is considered to be the best due to its high gluten content. It also gives pasta its appetizing warm yellow colour.

- **00 flour:** In Italy the fineness of the flour is graded 2, 1, 0 and 00, with 00 being the finest. This gold-standard flour, usually made from durum wheat, creates a delicate, silky pasta. Dough made with 00 flour can tear easily so needs careful handling.

- **Plain/all-purpose white flour:** Strong with high elasticity due to the gluten content.

- **Bread flour:** Due to its high gluten content, bread flour works well in thick pastas, such as lasagne sheets. Both bread flour and plain/all-purpose flour will go to mush if overcooked so keep an eye on it while it's in the pot.

- **Whole wheat flour:** This has a higher nutrition and lower carbohydrate content than white flour.

- **Rye flour:** Stronger tasting with a more robust texture than wheat flour.

- **Soy flour:** A low-carbohydrate flour but low in gluten so it produces pasta that breaks easily.

- **Almond flour:** This gluten-free flour is high in protein and nutrients but has a very low elasticity so try combining with another gluten-free flour such as tapioca starch.

- **Chickpea (gram) flour:** Low in calories, high in fibre with a nutty taste, gluten-free chickpea flour is easy to make at home by putting dried chickpeas through a food processor.

- **Buckwheat flour:** This low-calorie option is high in fibre and protein and gluten-free. Buckwheat pasta (pizzoccheri) has a wonderfully chewy texture.

- **Quinoa flour:** A healthy gluten-free option due to being low on the glycaemic index and high in protein and fibre.

PANGRATTATO DI PANE

Cooked and seasoned breadcrumbs are popular in southern Italy, particularly in Sicily. Breadcrumbs emerged as a quick way to transform stale or leftover bread and became known as the poor person's parmesan.

The bread is broken down into chunks or crumbs that are then coated in olive oil and gently toasted in a frying pan with whatever else is to hand. This could be pine nuts, garlic or anchovies, or herbs such as rosemary, thyme or basil. For extra oomph, chilli or lemon zest sometimes makes an appearance. Sweet flavourings such as sugar, cinnamon or nutmeg may also find their way into the mix.

While the breadcrumbs are crisping up, they absorb the flavours of the other ingredients and can then be used as a zingy topping for pasta dishes. They can also be stirred directly into the pasta itself to add a contrasting crunchy texture.

IN HEAVEN, AFTER ANTIPASTI, THE FIRST COURSE WILL BE PASTA.

Steve Albini

Cheeses to go with pasta

PARMESAN (PARMIGIANO-REGGIANO)

Whey and then rennet are added to unpasteurized cow's milk in great copper vats to form curds. These are then pressed into huge wheels, each weighing at least 40 kg (90 lbs).

The wheels are formed for a minimum of twelve months. During this time they develop a thick, seemingly impenetrable rind and the cheese acquires its tangy taste and rich yellow colour.

Parmesan is produced in many different areas of the world but can only carry the *Parmigiano-Reggiano* stamp if it has been made in Bologna, Reggio Emilia, Mantua, Modena or Parma: a cluster of cities known for their culture, grand architecture and fine cuisine.

A *stravecchio* stamp means that the cheese has been aged for three years and *stravecchione* tells you that it's over four years old. The older it is, the richer the taste will be. Parmesan is a key ingredient for many pasta recipes but it can also be grated to use as a topping or melted to a golden crisp on top of a pasta bake.

PECORINO ROMANO

This sheep's milk cheese has a strong bite and a grainy texture and, like parmesan, is made using rennet. Despite its paler colour and softer texture, which give it a gentler appearance, it has a sharp, tangy taste.

Once the wheels of pecorino cheese have been formed, a person known as a *salatore* rubs them with coarse salt every few days, then once a week until the cheese is fully matured, resulting in quite a salty taste.

Pecorino Romano is one of Italy's oldest cheeses. It dates back to Roman times and was an important staple for Roman soldiers. Until the end of the nineteenth century, it was only produced in the area surrounding Rome but a surge in demand led many producers to move their production to the rugged island of Sardinia where most pecorino cheese is still made today.

It is matured for a minimum of eight months and, like parmesan, it can be added to a sauce or grated as a topping.

FONTINA

This is a dense, mountain cheese made from cow's milk, with small holes and a warm, nutty flavour. Gruyère, Gouda or Emmental are good substitutes.

RICOTTA

This dazzling white, soft cheese is mild and creamy. It tastes and looks gorgeous combined with dark green vegetables such as spinach. It is made from the whey of cow's or goat's milk.

GORGONZOLA

A soft blue-veined cheese with a powerful taste, gorgonzola makes for a strong-tasting sauce.

CHEDDAR

This hard yellow cheese is from the south-west of England. Purists may throw up their hands in horror at the thought of using Cheddar for pasta dishes but in English speaking countries it's a hugely popular addition to macaroni cheese or grated on top of spaghetti bolognese.

PARMESAN FACTS

- Parmigiano-Reggiano, known as the "King of Cheeses", is accepted by Credem Bank, in Emilia-Romagna, as loan collateral. This helps local farmers with cash flow and saves them money on storage and a team of people maintain the wheels of cheese while they mature. After three years, the cheese, which has increased in value, is returned to the farmers. So far the bank has almost half a million wheels stashed away and calls this arrangement, "from cow to bank".

- Just 30 grams of parmesan contains up to 50 per cent of your recommended daily calcium intake.

- Parmesan was used as an ice-cream flavour among the upper classes of Georgian England.

- After 30 months of ageing, parmesan becomes lactose-free.

- The crystals that give parmesan that wonderful crunch are tyrosine, an amino acid.

- That tough rind can look a little scary, but you can save it and grate it into sauces.

Meats to cook with pasta

GUANCIALE

This meat-and-fat striped cheek of the pig has a rich taste
and buttery texture. When the strips or small chunks of
guanciale are heated, the fat melts into the pan, yielding
a rich flavour. This high fat content makes it a perfect
ingredient for carbonara and amatriciana.

It may be coated in a blend of aromatic herbs and
spices, mostly garlic, salt, pepper, rosemary, sage and
thyme. Tuscan *guanciale* uses a milder, more aromatic
blend of herbs. *Guanciale* from the Adriatic coast may be
smoked, and in Calabria, further south, it is more fiery.

PANCETTA

Guanciale can be difficult to get hold of outside Italy so
most recipes will call for pancetta instead. It has a more
robust and chewy texture than guanciale.

Fresh herbs to use with pasta

Dried herbs are readily available and it is useful to store them in your kitchen for those occasions when you need to give your sauce a quick lift.

Fresh ones, however, are a completely different beast and a very exciting one, too. The bright, aromatic flavours will really give your pasta sauces extra pzazz.

Fresh herbs will grow happily in pots on a warm sunny windowsill, ready for you to grab a handful when needed. Combine with a slosh of olive oil or melted butter and balance with a generous splash of something acidic such as tomato purée or lemon juice, and you can make a meal out of any pasta.

- **Basil:** Pungent, with a hint of mint: fresh basil and tomatoes are a match made in heaven so it's often used in tomato-based sauces. It loses its flavour once cooked so tear it into rough pieces and add to your sauce just before serving. It's also a punch-packing addition to pangrattato.

- **Chives:** Where onions and garlic go, chives will happily follow. Snip them into little pieces and either stir them into your sauce at the end or use them as a colourful garnish.

- **Flat-leaf (Italian) parsley:** This has a stronger taste than ruffled parsley. It is mildly peppery and also makes a great garnish.

- **Oregano:** Earthy oregano is synonymous with southern Italian cooking.

- **Thyme:** Aromatic and citrusy, thyme is gorgeous with creamy sauces. Use a knife to scrape the leaves off the sprig or else put the whole sprig in the sauce and fish it out before you eat.

- **Sage:** Sage has a pungent, slightly minty taste that can also be quite bitter. Throw a handful of fresh sage leaves into a pan of foaming butter, however, and they become crisp and subtly aromatic.

DID YOU KNOW?

Kneading pasta dough by hand is a strenuous task so when larger-scale production took off in Italy, teams of workers would use their feet to knead batches of dough. This made the job much easier but it would still take a "full day's walking" to get the dough just right.

PASTA IS PHENOMENAL. ONCE YOU'VE COOKED PASTA PROPERLY FOR THE FIRST TIME IT BECOMES SECOND NATURE.

Gordon Ramsay

Coloured and herb pasta

Here are some ideas for introducing a bit of wow to the basic dough recipes that we cover in the next chapter. Add beautiful colours to your home-made pasta by adding everyday vegetables to the dough. Purée your chosen vegetable either by hand or in a food processor and allow it to cool. Remove as much moisture as you can before adding to your pasta mixture: either drain through a sieve or squeeze by hand. You need a fairly dry pulp. Add just enough pulp to bring colour to the dough without making it go sticky. If your dough does become sticky, you can remedy it by adding a little more flour.

- **Carrots:** Peel and dice, then simmer with a dash of salt until tender and drain.

- **Beetroots:** Roast in the oven until tender. Alternatively, buy them ready-cooked.

- **Spinach:** Plunge handfuls of spinach into simmering water until the leaves turn dark green – usually less than a minute.

- **Fresh herbs:** With their distinctive aromas, fresh herbs make an exciting addition to fresh pasta. If you're using fresh herbs in the sauce, use the same ones in the pasta. A little goes a long way so you don't need much. Use wild garlic leaves or the popular Mediterranean herbs such as basil, thyme or oregano. Strip the leaves off first – any sharp or woody fragments will wreck your pasta dough and won't be much fun to eat. You can either crush the herbs very finely and add to the flour before preparing your dough, or sandwich the whole leaves between two thin pieces of rolled-out dough – basil has a particularly striking impact.

- If you want to be really creative, petals from **edible flowers** make a particularly beautiful addition.

As with the other pasta recipes, allow your dough to rest at room temperature for around 20 minutes before you roll it out.

Once rolled, allow around 10 minutes to dry before cutting into shapes.

PASTA
RECIPES

Both dried and fresh pasta are readily available but with a little basic knowledge and just a few ingredients you can easily tap into that authentic pasta-cooking experience.

This section is packed with inspiring recipes, beginning with instructions for basic pasta and gnocchi. We'll then move on to sauces, starting with the substantial dishes of the mountainous regions in the far north of Italy. Travelling down to Rome and then Naples and Sicily, we'll see the key ingredients change swiftly to tomatoes and olive oil. And no book about pasta would be complete without a recipe for macaroni cheese. This widely popular dish is of unclear origin so it appears at the end of the chapter.

A phrase that sometimes appears next to ingredients in Italian recipe books is *quanto basta*, meaning use "just enough" to get the flavour you need. This gives you the freedom to miss out anything you don't like and include more of what you love.

Conversions

The recipes in this chapter use metric measurements, but if you prefer using imperial (and you don't have a smartphone to do the conversions for you), here are some basic tables:

25 g ≈ 1 oz	15 ml ≈ ½ fl. oz
60 g ≈ 2 oz	30 ml ≈ 1 fl. oz
85 g ≈ 3 oz	75 ml ≈ 2½ fl. oz
115 g ≈ 4 oz	120 ml ≈ 4 fl. oz
255 g ≈ 9 oz	270 ml ≈ 9 fl. oz

DID YOU KNOW?

The world's largest bowl of pasta was made in Krakow, Poland, on 24 October 2015.

Forty chefs took over 19 hours to prepare the pasta, which weighed in at 7,900 kg (17,417 lb) and was served in a bowl 87 cm (34 in.) deep and 4.66 m (16 ft) in diameter.

This record-breaking bowl of pasta was made outside Krakow's Tauron Arena, and was served with bolognese sauce to over 10,000 people who were either watching or taking part in the city's annual half-marathon.

Basic pasta

A simple and versatile pasta recipe. Use this as a base to make any shape you like. See page 57 for the list of flours, including gluten-free ones.

Serves 4

INGREDIENTS

400 g semolina flour (or another flour of your choice)
1 tsp salt
Approx. 200 ml lukewarm water

METHOD

Combine the flour and salt in a large bowl. Gradually add the water and form a dough by hand. Alternatively, pulse it using a food processor until it resembles breadcrumbs. You may need less or more water than the quantity listed here. You are aiming for a non-sticky dough that is stiff yet malleable. It needs to be quite hard, which makes it more difficult to knead. Persevere until it stops cracking and it feels smooth and can be rolled into a ball.

Put it back in the bowl and leave to rest for 30 minutes. This allows the gluten to relax and it will be easier to roll out flat.

Divide the dough into four pieces and, if using a pasta machine, feed one piece through on the widest setting to create a sheet of pasta. (Cover the remaining ones with a damp tea towel to prevent drying out.) Fold over and repeat 6–8 times to work the dough. Between each feed, form it by hand into a rectangle, approximately 8 cm × 20 cm.

Finally, pass the dough through the machine on a narrower setting and, without folding, repeat the process, decreasing the setting each time.

Alternatively, using a rolling pin, follow the same fold-and-roll procedure as for the machine until your dough is the desired thickness: for example 1 mm thick for tagliatelle and 3 mm for ravioli.

Pass your rolled dough through the machine to create the shapes you want, or place it on a chopping board and use a sharp knife to cut the shapes out. Repeat with the other balls of dough.

Boil for 2–3 minutes.

Egg pasta

A smooth, silky pasta.

Serves 4

INGREDIENTS

300 g 00 flour
Pinch of salt
3 medium free-range eggs

METHOD

Combine the flour and salt in a bowl and make a well in the middle. Break the eggs into it and, with one hand, draw the flour over the eggs and into the centre. Mix until you can knead it into a ball of solid, elastic dough.

Wrap in cling film and refrigerate for 30 minutes.

Once out, allow the dough to reach room temperature then divide into four and either use a pasta machine or hand-roll one piece to the desired thickness. (Cover the remaining ones with a damp tea towel to prevent drying out.) Repeat with the other pieces of dough. Boil for 2–3 minutes.

Buckwheat pasta (pizzoccheri)

A sturdy buckwheat pasta, suitable for a gluten-free diet.

Serves 4

INGREDIENTS

240 g buckwheat flour
Pinch of salt
3 eggs

METHOD

Follow the same instructions as for the egg pasta on page 78, but cut it by hand.

When you're ready to cut the dough into strips, rather than laying it flat on the surface, roll it around the rolling pin and then carefully slide the rolling pin out and gently allow the rolled-up pasta to fold over on itself. This makes it easier to slice.

Let the pasta dry for 10 minutes before cooking.

Gnocchi

These warming potato dumplings from the Lombardy region pair beautifully with the simplest sauce.

Serves 4

INGREDIENTS

1 kg starchy white potatoes
320–350 g plain flour
2 tsp salt

METHOD

Boil the potatoes whole in salted water. Leave the skins on so they will absorb less water – you need them as dry as possible. When they are just soft, drain and leave to dry.

Meanwhile, combine the flour and salt.

Peel your potatoes while they are as hot as you can handle. The hotter they are, the lighter your gnocchi will be.

Mash the potatoes until lump-free and fluffy, then form into a heap on a floured work surface. Add the flour gradually. Knead into a soft dough, using just enough flour to hold the potatoes together. It should be non-sticky and able to hold its shape.

Dust the work surface with more flour. Pull off a handful of dough and roll it into a 2-cm thick sausage shape. Cut into 1–2-cm lengths and repeat with the rest of the dough.

To form the gnocchi shapes, rest a fork on the work surface, prongs upward. Dust one piece of dough with flour and roll it over the prongs to form the ridges. Peel it off the fork and gently pinch into that classic gnocchi shape. Lay each piece on a large, flour-dusted board or tray.

To cook, boil the gnocchi in a large saucepan of salted water for 2 minutes. They will bob to the surface when cooked.

Minestrone soup

A hearty soup for all times of year but especially for those cold winter nights. For a vegan version, swap the pancetta for another can of beans.

Serves 4

INGREDIENTS

A generous slug of olive oil

1 onion, very finely chopped

1 celery stick, very finely chopped

1 carrot, peeled and very finely chopped

100 g finely diced, smoked pancetta

2 garlic cloves, crushed

½ –1 tsp dried oregano

1 can cannellini beans

1 can chopped tomatoes

2 tbsp tomato purée

1.2 litres vegetable or chicken stock

1 bay leaf

Salt and pepper, to taste

80 g small pasta shapes of your choice

100 g greens – kale, Swiss chard, spinach, cavolo nero (or a mixture of these), roughly torn

A handful of basil, roughly torn, to serve

Finely grated parmesan, to serve

METHOD

Put the oil in a large saucepan over a low-medium heat and gently fry the onion, celery, carrot and pancetta to make a *soffritto* (base). Your soffritto is ready when all the ingredients have broken down and blended together. This should take 20–30 minutes.

Stir in the garlic and oregano, and cook for a further couple of minutes, taking care not to burn the garlic.

Add the beans, chopped tomatoes, tomato purée, stock and bay leaf, and simmer for 30–40 minutes.

Add salt and pepper to taste then tip the pasta in and continue to simmer. Add the greens just before the pasta reaches the al dente point, then cook for another couple of minutes.

Serve topped with the basil and parmesan.

Pizzoccheri with cabbage, potatoes and cheese

This mountain dish of buckwheat pasta is the star of the show in winter-warming stews from northern Italy.

Serves 4

INGREDIENTS

3–4 medium potatoes, cut into cubes

300 g pizzoccheri pasta

400 g leafy green vegetables, roughly torn[1]

130 g unsalted butter (or vegan butter substitute)

3–4 cloves of garlic, crushed

175 g fontina or Gruyère (or vegan) cheese, roughly chopped

Salt and pepper to taste

---

[1] Use any kind of cabbage or leafy vegetables. Savoy cabbage, Swiss chard and spinach provide an interesting combination of textures and tastes.

METHOD

Bring a large saucepan of salted water to the boil and add the potatoes. After a couple of minutes, add the pasta and boil for a further 10 minutes or so. Add your cabbage/leafy vegetables towards the end of the 10 minutes, depending on how well you like them cooked. They don't need long so you could add them while your garlic is cooking during the next step.

While the pasta and potatoes are boiling, fry the garlic in the butter very gently in a small frying pan. A couple of minutes should be enough. Remove from the heat and set aside.

Drain the pasta and vegetables then tip them back into the saucepan. Stir in the cheese and garlic butter to allow the cheese to melt.

Add salt and pepper to taste.

Serve straightaway to prevent the cheese going stringy.

Pumpkin and amaretti biscuit ravioli

A sweet yet tangy pasta dish, traditionally eaten at Christmas in the Lombardy region. Butternut squash works just as well as pumpkin.

Serves 4

INGREDIENTS

Pasta dough for 4 people

2 kg pumpkin (or squash), peeled, deseeded and cut into chunks

2 tbsp extra virgin olive oil

6 amaretti biscuits, crushed

1 tsp lemon juice

½ tsp ground ginger

¼ tsp cinnamon

Salt and pepper to taste

METHOD

Preheat the oven to 200°C (425°F) then place the pumpkin or squash chunks in a roasting tin, coat them with a little olive oil and roast until soft – around 20–25 minutes.

While the pumpkin cooks, roll the dough into thin sheets and leave to rest for 20–30 minutes.

When the pumpkin is soft, purée with a potato masher or food processor then return it to the tin and place in the still-warm oven for a minute or two to dry it out a little. Transfer to a mixing bowl, allow to cool, then combine with all the other ingredients.

Using either a knife or a ravioli cutter, cut the ravioli into squares: 6 cm x 6 cm is a good size. Place half the ravioli squares on a sheet of baking paper on a baking tray then put a small amount of the pumpkin mix in the middle of each square. Wet the edges of the squares with a little water and put another square on top of each. Use the prongs of a fork to press the top and bottom squares together. Alternatively, use a round pastry cutter. The ravioli only need a couple of minutes to cook in boiling water (they are done when they float to the surface). Delicious with olive oil, melted butter or sage butter (see page 67).

Lasagne

A classic favourite – cosy and filling.

Serves 4

INGREDIENTS

125 g pasta sheets (fresh or dried)
For the ragù:
1 tbsp olive oil
20 g butter
75 g pancetta, finely chopped
1 onion, finely chopped
1 carrot, finely chopped
1 stick of celery, finely chopped
275 g beef mince
175 g pork mince
A good slug of medium red wine
175 g passata di pomodoro
1 tbsp tomato purée
100 ml full-fat or soya milk
Salt and pepper

For the béchamel sauce:
30 g butter
30 g plain flour
400 ml full-fat or soya milk
Pinch of grated nutmeg (optional)
Salt and pepper
50–100 g parmesan, to serve

METHOD

To make the ragù:

Make a soffritto by cooking the chopped pancetta, onion, carrot and celery very gently in the oil and butter for half an hour, until the vegetables soften.

Stir in the minced meat and cook until brown.

Add the wine, simmer for a few minutes until it has reduced a little in volume, then add the passata and tomato purée.

Cover the pan and simmer gently for roughly 90 minutes. Add the milk a little at a time, during the cooking process, stirring regularly to ensure that the ragù doesn't burn. Season to taste.

To make the béchamel:
Gently warm the milk. In a different saucepan, gently melt the butter, then vigorously stir in the flour to make a paste before removing from the heat. Whisk in the milk, bit by bit. Add the nutmeg (if using) and a little salt and pepper. Return to the heat and simmer. Keep stirring for 5-10 minutes until the sauce resembles double cream. Both sauces need to be quite wet and loose to help the pasta cook, especially if you're using dried pasta.

Put it all together:
Heat the oven to 180°C (400°F)

If you're using dried pasta sheets, give them a dunk in boiling water for 2 or 3 minutes.

Grease an ovenproof dish with butter or olive oil and spread a dollop of ragù across the bottom of the dish. Add a layer of pasta sheets then a layer of béchamel sauce. Repeat until the dish is full and you have a layer of béchamel on the top.

Sprinkle with the parmesan and bake for 20-25 minutes until golden brown. (Prod with a fork to make sure that the pasta has cooked.)

Pesto

Fresh, green and herby, this sauce is fun to make.

Serves 4

INGREDIENTS

15 g pine nuts
1–2 cloves of garlic
Pinch of sea salt (rock or flaked)
50–60 g fresh basil leaves
80 ml extra virgin olive oil
35 g parmesan cheese, grated
15 g pecorino cheese, grated

METHOD

With a mortar and pestle, roughly pound the pine nuts, garlic and salt together then gradually introduce the basil and oil. If using a food processor, pulse the pine nuts, garlic and salt to a rough paste. Add the basil and oil and pulse again until you get the consistency you prefer. Stir in the cheese.

Cacio e pepe

A zesty, peppery dish that is quick and easy to prepare.

Serves 4

INGREDIENTS
400 g bucatini (or spaghetti)
160 g pecorino or vegan cheese
1–2 tsp ground black pepper
Pinch of salt

METHOD
Cook the pasta according to the packet instructions.

Combine the cheese and pepper in a bowl.

When the pasta is almost cooked, use a mug to scoop out some of the water and gradually spoon 4-6 tbsp of the pasta water into the cheese and pepper mixture. Blend in each spoonful vigorously until you get a thick sauce with a paste texture. Add salt to taste.

Drain the cooked pasta then transfer to the bowl of cheese sauce and mix together.

Alla gricia

A tangy dish with a rich, silky texture.

Serves 4

INGREDIENTS

400 g bucatini, spaghetti, rigatoni or penne

200 g guanciale or pancetta (this will need 1–2 tbsp of olive oil) cut into 4-mm strips

Black pepper, ground

120 g pecorino cheese, finely grated

Salt to taste

METHOD

Cook the pasta according to the instructions on the packet.

Gently heat the guanciale or pancetta and olive oil until the meat turns light brown and crispy.

When your pasta is cooked, stir into the meat and season with the pepper. Quickly stir in roughly two-thirds of the cheese then stir in a few tablespoons of the pasta water. Serve with the remainder of the cheese and black pepper.

DID YOU KNOW?

On April Fools' Day 1957, the BBC featured a family in Switzerland harvesting a "spaghetti tree".

At that time the consumption of pasta in UK households was mostly limited to tinned spaghetti in tomato sauce. Not much was known about authentic pasta, which would have been considered very exotic, so many viewers believed the story. Tempted by the idea of growing their own spaghetti tree, people contacted the BBC to ask how they might do so.

The BBC's response was to suggest that they "place a sprig of spaghetti in a tin of tomato sauce and hope for the best".

YOU CAN BUY A GOOD
PASTA BUT WHEN YOU
COOK IT YOURSELF IT
HAS ANOTHER FEELING.

Agnes Varda

Carbonara

This universally loved "bacon and egg" style pasta dish is both substantial and satisfying.

Serves 4

INGREDIENTS

400 g spaghetti

Extra virgin olive oil

3 large eggs

3 large egg yolks

50 g pecorino cheese, 50 g parmesan cheese, finely grated and mixed together

2–3 cloves garlic, whole

300–400 g pancetta, cut into small strips

Black pepper

Sprig of parsley (optional)

METHOD

Cook the spaghetti according to the instructions on the packet.

Using a fork, combine the whole eggs, egg yolks and half the pecorino and parmesan cheese in a bowl, then season with pepper.

Heat a couple of tablespoons of olive oil over a medium-high heat and give the garlic cloves a few bashes (no need to completely crush them). Cook for a couple of minutes to release the flavour then remove them from the oil. Add the pancetta and cook until crispy.

Drain the spaghetti but keep back a little of the cooking water.

Add the spaghetti to the pancetta pan, together with a ladle of the spaghetti water, and give a brisk stir to combine the ingredients.

Toss in the egg and cheese mixture. Your pan must be at the right temperature for this step: too cold and the egg won't cook; too hot and the egg will scramble. It's best to remove the pan from the heat and allow to cool for a minute or so before adding the egg and cheese. You can also stir in another splash of spaghetti water at this stage.

Heap the spaghetti into bowls and top with the remaining cheese mixture and add black pepper.

Amatriciana

A warm and spicy tomato sauce with the tang of pecorino.
Usually eaten with bucatini.

Serves 4

INGREDIENTS

400 g bucatini (or spaghetti)

Extra virgin olive oil

125 g guanciale, chopped into small pieces (or
  pancetta with a couple of extra slugs of olive oil)

½ large onion, finely chopped

1–2 cloves of garlic, crushed

75 ml white wine

2 x 400 g cans chopped tomatoes or 800 g fresh
  tomatoes, peeled and chopped (if using fresh,
  use the ripest, juiciest ones you can find)

½ –1 tsp chilli flakes

½ tsp sugar

30–50 g pecorino cheese, finely grated

Salt and pepper to taste

METHOD

Sauté the guanciale or pancetta in a saucepan on a medium-high heat (if using pancetta, add a little oil). When the meat is cooked and crispy, scoop it out onto a plate. If you're using guanciale, add some oil now and on a lower heat, gently fry the onion. When it's soft, add the garlic and fry for another minute.

Add the wine and turn the heat up. When the wine has reduced to half its volume, add the tomatoes, chilli flakes and sugar and simmer for approximately half an hour. Give it the occasional stir and add salt and pepper to taste. When you have rich tomatoey sauce, stir in the guanciale or pancetta. At this point, another glug of olive oil will give your sauce an extra silky texture.

Cook the pasta according to the packet instructions. Before draining, add a few spoonfuls of the cooking water to the sauce, then combine it with the pasta. Serve with the grated pecorino.

Neapolitan sugo di pomodoro (tomato sauce)

In southern Italy tomato-based sauces are the classic accompaniment to pasta. This easy to make, tangy sauce is perfect for summer evenings.

Serves 4

INGREDIENTS

2 tbsp olive oil

2 medium onions, chopped

3 garlic cloves, crushed

1 tbsp tomato purée

2 x 400 g cans of chopped tomatoes or 800 g of fresh tomatoes, peeled and chopped (if using fresh, use the ripest, juiciest ones you can find)

1 tbsp sugar

A good slug of red wine (optional)

Pinch of salt and black pepper

Handful of fresh basil leaves, roughly torn (optional)

METHOD

Heat the olive oil in a large saucepan and gently cook the onions until soft and transparent. Add the garlic and soften by cooking very gently for a few minutes. Don't let the onions or garlic turn brown.

Add the remaining ingredients apart from the basil (if using) and bring to a high heat.

Cook for 30-45 minutes until your sauce is dark and concentrated. Keep an eye on it and stir regularly to prevent it sticking. Add the fresh basil at the end if desired.

This perky sauce pairs well with larger pasta shapes such as conchiglie, fusilli or penne.

Pangrattato – herby breadcrumbs

Pangrattato is a fabulous way of using up stale bread and adds crunch and flavour to most pasta dishes. Sprinkle over the top before serving.

Serves 4

INGREDIENTS

200–300 g stale bread

A generous slug of extra virgin olive oil

1–2 cloves of garlic, chopped in half

2–3 anchovies

Either a pinch of chilli flakes or 2 whole red chillies

Pinch of sea salt

Few twists of coarse black pepper

2–3 tsp lemon zest, finely grated

Few sprigs of your favourite herbs, washed, thoroughly dried and finely chopped

METHOD

Either grate the bread or put it through a food processor to make the breadcrumbs – you can have them fine or leave them fairly coarse, but the finer they are, the more seasoning they will soak up.

Gently heat the oil in a large frying pan and put in the garlic pieces and anchovies. If using whole chillies, add those now. Taking care not to let these ingredients burn, cook for a minute or so to release their flavour then remove from the oil.

Add the breadcrumbs and gently toast them until golden brown. They will eagerly soak up the oil so stir them briskly to ensure even absorption. Again, keep an eye on them to make sure they don't burn.

As they are just beginning to turn golden, remove from the heat, add the chopped herbs, lemon zest, optional chilli flakes and salt and pepper, then put back on the heat for another minute, tossing and stirring to combine the ingredients. Turn off the heat and let your pangrattato cool in the pan. Refrigerate leftovers in an air-tight container. They will last for a week or so. Restore the crunch by heating them on a baking tray at a low temperature.

Sugo alla puttanesca

This bold and piquant sauce from Naples is quick to prepare and is traditionally served with spaghetti.

Serves 4

INGREDIENTS

400 g spaghetti

3 tbsp olive oil

1 onion, finely chopped

3–4 large garlic cloves, crushed

Pinch of chilli, either flakes or powder (optional)

Pinch of salt

2 x 400 g cans of chopped tomatoes

A generous squirt of tomato purée

4–6 anchovy fillets, finely chopped

120 g pitted black olives

2–3 tbsp capers

METHOD

Cook the spaghetti according to the instructions on the packet.

Meanwhile, heat the oil in a large, deep frying pan and gently fry the onion until it turns transparent. Add the garlic and cook on a low heat for a few minutes. If using chilli, add it now and cook a little longer. Don't let the onions or garlic burn.

Stir in the rest of the ingredients. At this point, you can add a few tablespoons of the pasta water. Simmer gently until the sauce has reduced in volume – usually around 15 minutes.

Drain the spaghetti and toss with the sauce.

Season to taste.

Tip: this is one recipe you can play around with to your heart's content. Add pine nuts, tuna, artichoke hearts – anything you like. It might not be "true" Neapolitan puttanesca but it will still be delicious. For a more intense flavour, use anchovy oil in place of olive oil.

Spaghetti alle vongole

Originating from Naples, spaghetti with clams is very popular throughout the southern region of Campania. Enjoy the *rosso* version (with tomatoes) or *bianco* (without).

Serves 4

INGREDIENTS

1 kg fresh clams in shells

400 g spaghetti

Extra virgin olive oil

2–4 cloves of garlic, chopped

1 medium to large red chilli, finely chopped

175–200 ml dry white wine

6–8 cherry tomatoes, cut in half (if cooking the rosso version)

Handful of chopped parsley

Salt and pepper to taste

METHOD

Clean the clams by soaking them in a bowl of cold, salted water for 20 minutes. Discard any that are open or open up during the soaking process. Remove them from the water, refill the bowl with clean, salted water and soak for another 20 minutes. Give them a good scrub with a brush then repeat the soaking process.

Cook the spaghetti according to the instructions.

While the pasta is cooking, warm the olive oil in a large pan and gently fry the garlic and chilli until you can smell the garlic. Add the wine and clams, stir and cover the pan. Cook until the clams open up – usually 3–5 minutes. If you're going for the rosso version, throw your tomatoes in now. When the pasta is cooked, drain it and combine it with the clams, add the parsley and salt and pepper if needed, then toss everything together.

Spaghetti all'assassina

From Bari, in the heel of Italy, this dish translates as "killer spaghetti". The spaghetti is cooked risotto-style in the sauce, giving it an intense flavour and unexpected crunch.

Serves 4

INGREDIENTS

8 tbsp extra virgin olive oil

6 cloves of garlic, crushed

1–2 hot red chillies, finely chopped (discard the seeds if you want a milder heat)

400 g dried spaghettini or fine spaghetti

1 litre of passata

A generous squirt of red pepper purée

500 ml–1 litre of water

½–1 tsp sugar (optional)

Salt and pepper to taste

6–8 tomatoes, halved and sautéed (optional)

METHOD

Using a large frying pan, warm the olive oil to a medium heat and add the garlic, chillies and spaghetti or spaghettini. Cook for a few minutes and keep the ingredients moving, ensuring the garlic doesn't turn brown.

Combine the passata, water and tomato purée in a jug then gradually add it to the pan, stirring occasionally, allowing the spaghetti to caramelize as you turn it. Add seasoning now if you feel it is necessary, and sugar if you want to temper the acidity of the tomatoes. If you're adding cherry tomatoes, stir those in at the end.

You are aiming for pasta that is cooked yet crunchy and a little bit burnt in places. Once cooked, serve immediately.

Prawn linguine

A light pasta dish perfect for summer evenings accompanied with a salad and a glass of dry white wine.

Serves 4

INGREDIENTS

400 g linguine

120 ml extra virgin olive oil

2–3 cloves garlic, finely chopped

1 medium red chilli, deseeded and finely chopped

200 ml dry white wine

400 g uncooked whole prawns

3 spring onions, chopped

3 medium tomatoes, skinned and chopped

3 stems of flat-leaf parsley, chopped

Handful of basil leaves, roughly torn

Salt and black pepper to taste

1 lemon, quartered, to serve

METHOD

Cook the pasta according to pack instructions.

Heat the olive oil in a large frying pan over a medium heat and add the garlic and chilli.

Fry gently for approximately 1 minute then add the spring onions and tomatoes.

Cook on the same heat for a couple of minutes then add the wine.

Allow to simmer until the wine has reduced to about a third in volume, then add the prawns and cook until they turn pink (around 2–3 minutes).

Drain the pasta and add to the pan of prawns. Add the parsley and toss everything together.

Add the basil leaves, season with salt and pepper, and pile into serving dishes.

Serve with lemon wedges.

Sicilian pasta alla Norma

From Catania, a Sicilian city at the foot of volatile Mount Etna, this dish is named after the tragic heroine of the opera *Norma*, by the city's famous composer, Bellini.

Serves 4

INGREDIENTS

400 g spaghetti or a chunky pasta such as rigatoni

2 medium aubergines

200 ml extra virgin olive oil

Salt

1 medium onion, chopped

2–3 garlic cloves, crushed

400 g can chopped tomatoes

¼–½ tsp dried red chilli flakes

½–1 tsp dried oregano

A handful of fresh basil leaves, torn

50 g salted ricotta, parmesan or pecorino cheese (or vegan alternative), grated

METHOD

Cook the pasta according to pack instructions.

Chop the aubergines into medium-sized chunks (leave the skin on) then fry them on a low heat in olive oil until they turn golden – usually around 10 minutes. Give them a sprinkle of salt while they're frying.

Remove from the oil and set to one side.

Fry the onion on a low heat until translucent then add the garlic and fry for a further minute. (You might need to add more olive oil as aubergines have a habit of soaking it all up.)

Stir in the tomatoes, chilli flakes and oregano and simmer for around 10–15 minutes to reduce the sauce.

Add the aubergines and pasta and stir in approximately half a ladleful of the cooking water.

Spoon the pasta into bowls and top with the basil leaves and grated cheese.

LEMON GRANITA

Traditionally served at breakfast, this frozen drink from Sicily can be enjoyed at any time of day and is super-easy to make. It's a lovely refreshing drink that you could serve alongside a pasta meal, or even as a dessert.

- Combine 1 litre of water and 500 g of caster sugar in a bowl.

- Stir until the sugar has completely dissolved (you may need to heat it gently).

- Add the juice of 6-7 unwaxed lemons and, if you like, the zest of a couple of lemons for extra bite. Place the bowl in the freezer and every half hour or so, give the granita a mash up with a fork to prevent it from freezing solid. You will be rewarded with a mound of glittering crystals with a refreshing lemony zing.

- Spoon into large glasses and garnish with a sprig of mint.

IT'S A COMFORT TO
FIND PASTA IN THE
CUPBOARD AND GARLIC
AND PARSLEY IN
THE GARDEN.

Alice Waters

Pasta con le sarde

A surprisingly sweet and salty sardine pasta dish from Sicily.

Serves 4

INGREDIENTS

1 medium bulb of fennel, cored and finely
  chopped

400 g spaghetti

3–4 tbsp extra virgin olive oil

1 onion, sliced

1–1½ tsp fennel seeds, toasted

70 g pine nuts, lightly toasted

50 g currants

3–4 cloves garlic, crushed

4 anchovies, chopped (optional)

Slug of dry white wine

240 g sardines, drained

Zest of 1 orange

Zest of 1 lemon

A splash of juice from the orange and the lemon
Pepper to taste
Extra virgin olive oil, to drizzle

METHOD

Boil the chopped fennel for 5 minutes to soften it, then drain.

Cook the spaghetti until it is al dente, following the instructions on the packet.

Gently sauté the onion, fennel, fennel seeds, pine nuts, currants, garlic and anchovies (if using) in olive oil until the onion is translucent and the fennel is fully soft.

Pour in the wine and turn the heat up. When the mixture has reduced a little in volume, turn the heat down.

Add the sardines, the zest and a splash of juice from the fruit and cook for a few more minutes. To avoid breaking up the sardines, minimize stirring at this point.

Add pepper to taste.

Drain the pasta and gently stir into the mixture, then heap into bowls and drizzle with more olive oil.

Oven-baked macaroni cheese

A pasta and cheese dish was first recorded in a fourteenth-century Italian cookery book and over time has evolved into the richly cheesy dish we love today.

Serves 4

INGREDIENTS

300 g macaroni

30 g butter (or vegan butter substitute)

25 g flour

500 ml full-fat or soya milk

1 tsp Dijon or English mustard (optional)

200–250 g strong Cheddar or vegan cheese, grated

Salt and pepper to taste

METHOD

Preheat the oven to 220°C (475°F).

Prepare the macaroni according to the instructions but remove from the heat when it is a little less cooked than normal – probably around 8–10 minutes.

While the macaroni cooks, melt the butter in a medium saucepan. Don't let the butter burn.

When it starts to foam, gradually add the flour, stirring constantly. Reduce the heat and add the milk, bit by bit, stirring briskly to prevent the sauce from becoming lumpy. If lumps do form, give it a good go with a whisk.

If adding mustard, salt and/or pepper, do that now, then remove the sauce from the heat and stir in half the cheese.

Drain the pasta, stir in a few tablespoons of the cooking water to the sauce, then combine the pasta with the sauce.

Pour the mixture into a shallow ovenproof dish and top with the rest of the cheese. Bake in the oven for 10 minutes until the top is brown and crispy.

Perfect partners

You've chosen your sauce and pasta. Now you need a gorgeous wine to bring out the best in your culinary creation.

Here are some basic rules of thumb for choosing wines and, on the following three pages, suggestions for wines to partner with the various pasta dishes.

- Pair your wine with the dominant flavours of the sauce. For example, if herbs are the main focus of the dish, as with pesto for example, choose a herby wine.

- If you've used wine to cook the sauce, serving the same wine at the table will echo the flavour.

- Choose a wine similar in weight to the dish: heavy wines go with heavy sauces, light wines go with delicate sauces.

- "What grows together, goes together" is a good rule of thumb, so, if possible, select a wine from the same region as the sauce.

—● Italian wines tend to be high in acidity making them perfect for many of the sauces that go with pasta.

TOMATO-BASED SAUCES

Either a red or white wine is suitable for this type of sauce but it should be able to stand up to the acidity of the tomatoes. Choose a fresh-tasting wine high in acidity such as a Verdicchio, a sweet white with a complex aromatic flavour, or Nero d'Avola (also known as Calabrese), a fruity red from Sicily.

TOMATO AND MEAT SAUCES

Pair heavier dishes such as lasagne, bolognese or ravioli with a medium or full-bodied red wine that is robust enough to cut through the high fat content while complementing the rich flavours. Again, Nero d'Avola is a good choice, as is Cabernet Sauvignon, which is full-bodied and darkly fruity. Alternatively, Montepulciano, a medium-bodied red, is strong and peppery and goes well with any tomato-based sauce.

CHEESE-BASED SAUCES

If your macaroni cheese or alfredo is a bit heavy, choose something fairly refreshing to wash it down. A Chilean Pinot Noir, with its spicy notes and fruity flavours, has enough acidity to cut through the fat.

SEAFOOD PASTA

White wines are traditionally served with seafood but reds are also suitable. Soave is a smooth white wine from the Veneto region around Verona. It carries just the slightest hint of salinity, making it a perfect match for seafood dishes and anything containing garlic and oil. Pinot Grigio, a light and dry white, is also a good choice. If you prefer red, try a light, dry Pinot Noir.

PESTO PASTA

Both red and white wine can be paired with pesto but it needs a wine that is distinctive enough to complement the herby pungency of the pesto without clashing with it. A rich Chardonnay will bring out the creaminess of the parmesan. A bright, zingy Sauvignon Blanc or a Pinot Noir will complement this herby sauce.

THE ROMAN QUARTET: CACIO E PEPE, GRICIA, AMATRICIANA AND CARBONARA

The high tannin content of Montepulciano, a medium-bodied red, pairs beautifully with the generous helpings of parmesan in these dishes. Alternatively, the slight bitterness of Cortese di Gavi, a light, dry aromatic white, will enhance their creaminess.

Final Word

As our pasta journey draws to a close, we have seen how with just a few basic kitchen ingredients this popular staple can be transformed into a range of tasty dishes, most of which are not complicated or time-consuming to prepare.

If you would like to learn more about the history of pasta or if you would like more recipes, see the short list of resources on the next page.

Hopefully, this book has whetted your appetite and you're already deciding which recipe you'd like to try first: a simple, tongue-tingling cacio e pepe, possibly; or maybe you'd like to bring a touch of Naples into your home with a piquant spaghetti puttanesca.

Whichever you choose, enjoy your pasta adventures and have fun adapting these dishes to suit your own tastes.

BUON APPETITO!

Resources

BOOKS

Pasta Grannies: The Secrets of Italy's Best Home Cooks, Vicky Bennison (2019)

An A–Z of Pasta, Rachel Roddy (2021)

Homemade Pasta Made Simple: A Pasta Cookbook with Easy Recipes & Lessons to Make Fresh Pasta Any Night, Manuela Zangara (2017)

DOCUMENTARY

Stanley Tucci: Searching for Italy, CNN and BBC

WEBSITES

https://www.the-pasta-project.com/

https://www.washingtonpost.com/food/2022/05/09/pasta-shapes-guide-sauces

THE LITTLE BOOK OF
CURRY

Rufus Cavendish

Paperback
ISBN: 978-1-80007-417-0

From rogan josh and rendang to bunny chow and vindaloo, dive into this celebration of one of the world's most popular dishes: curry. Including the history of curry around the world, tips on growing your own spices, delicious recipes you can cook yourself and much more, *The Little Book of Curry* will help you spice up your life one dish at a time.

THE LITTLE BOOK OF
SUSHI

Rufus Cavendish

Paperback
ISBN: 978-1-80007-840-6

From seaweed-wrapped maki rolls to tuna-topped nigiri, dive into this celebration of one of the world's favourite dishes. Including the history of sushi, a tour of its biggest names, delicious recipes and much more, *The Little Book of Sushi* will be your handy guide to the bite-sized delicacy that has found favour all over the world.

Have you enjoyed this book?
If so, find us on Facebook at
SUMMERSDALE PUBLISHERS, on Twitter at
@SUMMERSDALE and on Instagram and TikTok at
@SUMMERSDALEBOOKS and get in touch.
We'd love to hear from you!

WWW.SUMMERSDALE.COM

IMAGE CREDITS

Cover and icon throughout – pasta bowl
© Alemoncz/Shutterstock.com; p.22 – pasta
shapes © Anatolir/Shutterstock.com